Let's hop into
this book ...

First Publication 2025 by Jenny Dyer

For further information
contact through facebook pages

Walking with Wildlife
and
JD's Snaps and Designs

Text and photographs © Jennifer Dyer 2024

ISBN 978-1-7637939-2-7

Cover and Artwork: Jenny Dyer

Can you count the animals?

Walking
with Wildlife

BOOK 3 - CAN YOU COUNT THE ANIMALS?

Written and photographed
by Jenny Dyer

One cuddly koala sitting in a tree.

Two kangaroos watching me.

Three cackling kookaburras perched on a branch.

Four noisy miners wishing they could dance.

Five flying ibises up in the sky.

**Six rainbow lorikeets
shouldn't eat pie.**

Seven lazy lizards
lying in the sun.

Eight plumed whistling ducks having fun.

Nine double-barred finches for you to see.

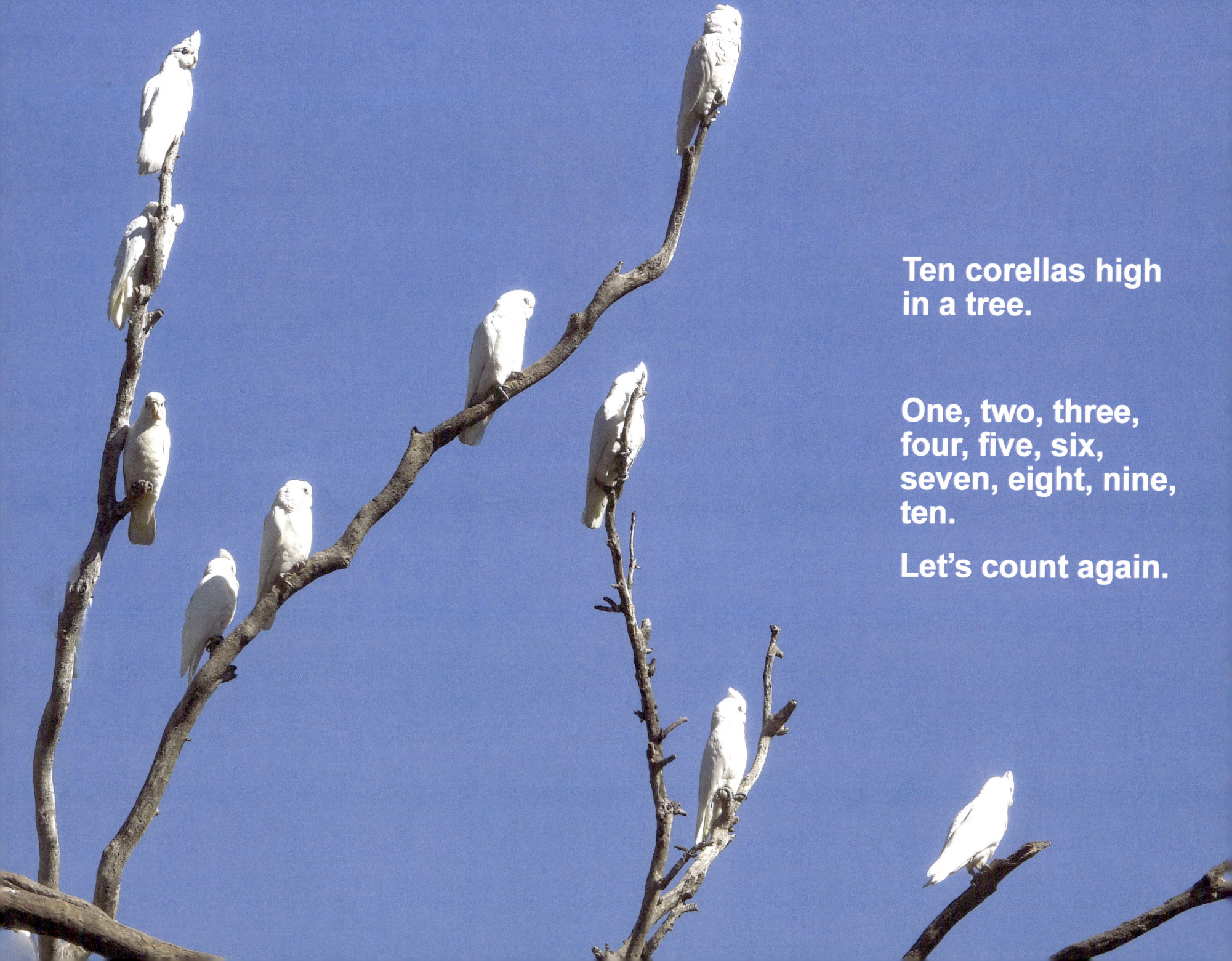

Ten corellas high in a tree.

One, two, three, four, five, six, seven, eight, nine, ten.

Let's count again.

How many animals can there be?

Koala

Kangaroo

Kookaburra

Noisy Miners

Ibis

Rainbow Lorikeet

Lizards

Plumed Whistling Duck

Double-barred finch

Corella

Let's count and you will see.

Sometimes they are just too hard to count!

Scan the code to find out why rainbow lorikeets shouldn't eat pies.

This is a female Golden Orb-weaver.

How many legs does a spider have?

How many insects can you see?
How many legs does an insect have?

www.ingramcontent.com/pod-product-compliance
Lightning Source LLC
Chambersburg PA
CBRC091226020426
42333CB00010B/82